Kid's Box

New Generation

Caroline Nixon &
Michael Tomlinson

CAMBRIDGE

Student's Book
with eBook
American English

Language summary

	Key vocabulary	**Key language**	**Sounds and spelling**
1 Hi! page 4	**Character names:** Mr. Star, Mrs. Star, Sally, Scott, Suzy, Marie, Maskman, Monty, Eva **Numbers:** 1–10 **Colors:** blue, green, pink, purple, red, orange, yellow, rainbow	**Greetings:** Hi. Goodbye. **Question words:** What's your name? I'm (Sally). How old are you? I'm (five).	**Initial letter sound:** r (red)
2 My school page 10	**School:** book, chair, eraser, pen, pencil, table **Character names:** Alex, Robert	**Question words:** Who's that? That's (Alex). How old is he/she? He's/She's (seven). Is he/she (six)? Yes, he/she is. / No, he/she isn't. How are you? I'm fine, thank you.	**Initial letter sounds:** p and b (pen, bag)

Marie's art: What happens when you mix colors?   page 16   **Trevor's values:** Make friends   page 17

	Key vocabulary	**Key language**	**Sounds and spelling**
3 Favorite toys page 18	**Toys:** ball, bike, car, computer, doll, drum, train **Colors:** black, brown, gray, white	**Question words:** What's your favorite toy? My favorite toy's my (drum). **Prepositions of place:** in, next to, on, under Where's your (ball)? It's (under) the (table). Is (the ball on the chair)? Yes, it is. / No, it isn't.	**Consonant sounds:** t and d (toy, doll)
4 My family page 24	**Family:** brother, sister, father, mother, grandfather, grandmother	**Adjectives:** beautiful, happy, sad, old, young, ugly He's/She's (happy). We're (young).	**Short vowel sound:** a (hat)

Marie's science: Which planets are near Earth?   page 30   **Trevor's values:** Be kind   page 31

Review: units 1, 2, 3, and 4   page 32

	Key vocabulary	**Key language**	**Sounds and spelling**
5 Our pets page 34	**Animals:** bird, cat, dog, fish, horse, mouse	**Adjectives:** big, small, clean, dirty, long, short It's (long). They're (dirty).	**Short vowel sound:** e (hen)
6 My face page 40	**The body and face:** ear, eye, face, hair, head, knees, mouth, nose, shoulders, toes, tooth/teeth	*Have* for possession: Do you have (big ears)? Yes, I do. / No, I don't. I have (black hair).	**Consonant sounds:** t and th (tooth, three)

Marie's science: How do we use our senses?   page 46   **Trevor's values:** Take care of pets   page 47

1 Hi!

1 🎧 2–3 **Listen and point. Listen and repeat.**

Mr. Star

Mrs. Star

Scott

Suzy

Sally

2 **Point and say the name.**

Sally

Vocabulary presentation 1: character names | **Language presentation 1:** greetings and question words

1 🎧 4 **Listen and do the actions.**

Maskman   Marie   Monty

2 🎵🎧 5 **Listen and say the chant.**

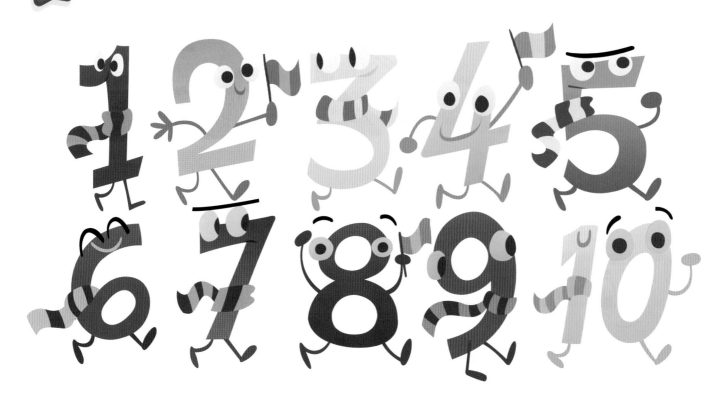

1 🎧 6 ▶ Listen and point.

2 🎧 7 Listen and repeat.

1  8–9 ▶ **Listen and sing. Do karaoke.**

Red and yellow and 🎨 and green.
Orange and purple and 🎨.
I can sing a 🌈.

2 🎧 10 **Listen and say the color.**

Monty's sounds and spelling

1 🎧 11 ▶ **Watch and say.**

A red robot on a rainbow.

2 **Look, find, and count.**

Red birds.

Six!

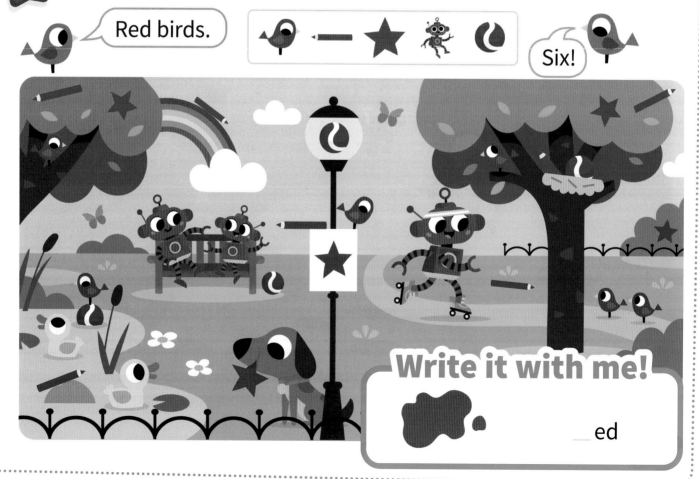

Write it with me!

_____ed

 ∩ 12 ▶ **Watch the video.**

 Act out the story.

Story: unit language in context　　9

2 My school

1 🎧 13–14 **Listen and point.**
Listen and repeat.

chair

table

book

eraser

pencil

pen

2 **Play and say.**   Pen.   It's blue.

Vocabulary presentation: school

 **1** ♪🎧 15 **Listen and say the chant.**

A ✏️ , a 📘 , an ⬜ , a ▭ ,
A 🟫 , a 🪑 . Say it again!

 **2** 🎧 16 **Listen and correct.**

Four purple chairs.

No. Six orange chairs.

Vocabulary practice: school   **11**

1 🎧 17-18 ▶ Listen and point. Listen and repeat.

That's Eva. She's eight.

Who's that?

Robert

Alex

2 Point, ask, and answer.

Who's that?

Eva.

She's eight.

Language presentation and practice 1: question words *Who's that? That's (Robert). How old is he/she? He's/She's (seven).*

 🎵🎧 19-20 ▶ Listen and sing. Do karaoke.

_____ Star, _____ Star, how are you?
I'm fine, thank you. I'm fine, thank you.
How are you?

Project

Make the puppets.

1 🎧 21 ▶ **Watch and say.**

Put the pizza in the purple bag.

2 **Look, point, and say.**

Seven pink books.

Write it with me!

_ag   _izza

1 🎧 22 ▶ **Watch the video.**

2 **Act out the story.**

Marie's art

What happens when you mix colors?

1 ▶ **Watch and answer.**

2 🎧 23 **Listen and look. Say the colors.**

Primary colors

Secondary colors

3 **Look, say, and check (✓).**

1   + = ✓    ☐

2   + = ☐    ☐

3   + = ☐   ☐

4   + = ☐   ☐

Red is the first primary color a baby can see.

Fact

Project

Make a color wheel.

Trevor's values

Make friends

Listen and point.

2 🎧 25 **Listen and say the number. Act it out.**

Language: *Are you OK? Come on! Let's play!* | emotional development

17

3 Favorite toys

1 🎧 26–27 **Listen and point. Listen and repeat.**

- doll
- drum
- computer
- car
- ball
- bike
- train

2 **Ask and answer.**

What's this?

It's a car.

 Listen and say the chant.

Black, brown, white, gray.
Look, listen, point, and say.

 Listen and say the number.

2 **Ask and answer.**

1 ♫🎧 32–33 ▶ **Listen and sing. Do karaoke.**

2 **Ask and answer.**

Is Monty under the chair?   No, he isn't.

Language practice: prepositions of place *Is (Monty) in / on / under / next to the (toy box)?*   21

1 🎧 34 ▶ Watch and say.

A doll, a drum, and a teddy bear on a train.
Drive under two tables!

2 Look and say.

A train on the table.

Number one.

Write it with me!

 _able   _rum

1 35 ▶ Watch the video.

2 36 Listen and say "yes" or "no."

4 My family

grandfather

grandmother

brother

sister

mother

father

2 **Point and say.**

Who's this?

Grandmother!

24   Vocabulary presentation: family

1 🎧 39 Listen and say the number.

2 🎧 40 Look, listen, and say.

 **Listen and sing. Do karaoke.**

He's my 🧑. She's my 👧.

She's my 🧒. And he's my 🧑.

We are family.

Listen and say the chant.

monty's sounds and spelling

1 🎧 46 ▶ **Watch and say.**

A sad cat on a mat. A happy cat in a black hat.

2 **Play and say.**

He's happy. He's next to a hat.

Grandfather!

Write it with me!

h _ t

🎧 47 ▶ **Watch the video.**

2 🎧 48 **Listen and say the number.**

Marie's science

Which planets are near Earth?

1 Watch and answer.

2 🎵 49 Listen, point, and say.

Mercury · Earth · Jupiter · Uranus

the sun

Venus · Mars · Saturn · Neptune

3 Color and say.

Earth

Mars

Neptune

Fact

Earth has one moon.
Jupiter has 79 moons.

Project

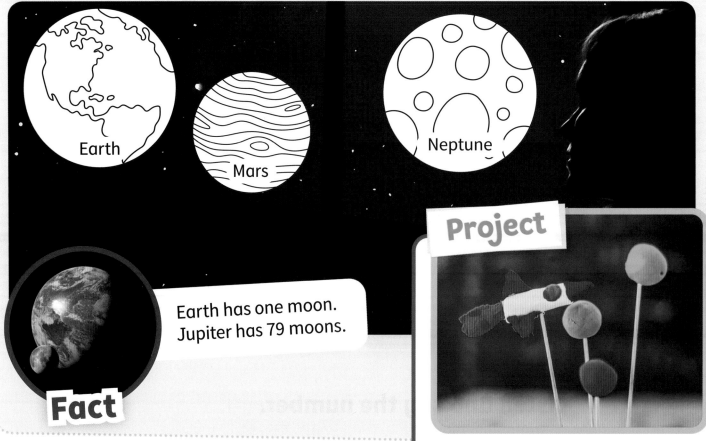

Make a planet.

Trevor's values

Be kind

 2 🎧 51 **Listen again and act it out.**

Language: *Here you are. Thanks. I'm sorry. That's OK.* | emotional development

 Review Units 1, 2, 3, and 4

1 🎧 52 **Listen and say the number.**

2 **Say and guess.**

It's pink. It's in a bag.

Number four.

∩ 53 **Listen and color. Make a spinner.**

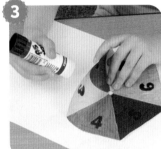

 Play the game.

5 Our pets

horse

The Star House
PET SHOW

fish

cat

mouse

bird

dog

2 **Say and guess.**   Suzy.   It's a dog.

Listen and say the chant. 🎵🎧 56

5

My horse is beautiful. My dog is too.
My fish is ugly. My bird is blue.

🎧 57 Listen and say "yes" or "no."

dirty

clean

small

long

big

short

2 Ask and answer.

What's long and gray?

The pencil.

Language presentation: adjectives *It's (clean). They're (dirty).*

 🎵 60 **Listen and do the actions.**

2 🎵🎧 61–62 ▶ **Listen and sing. Do karaoke.**

1 🎧 63 ▶ **Watch and say.**

A red pet hen on a nest with friends!

2 **Ask and answer.**

Where's the pink hen?

It's on the dog.

Write it with me!

h _ n

1 🎧 64 ▶ **Watch the video.**

 2 **Act out the story.**

Story: unit language in context   39

6 My face

1 🎧 65–66 **Listen and point. Listen and repeat.**

ear

hair

face

eye

nose

mouth

teeth

2 **Play and say.** Nose. It's here!

Vocabulary presentation: the face

 🎵🎧 67 **Listen and say the chant.**

Head, shoulders, knees and toes, knees and toes.

2 🎧 68 **Listen and correct.**

I'm a boy monster.

No. You're a girl monster.

Vocabulary presentation and practice: the body and face   41

1 🎧 69–70 ▶ **Listen and point. Listen and repeat.**

2 **Play and say.**

Language presentation: *have for possession Do you have (a small mouth)? I have (pink hair).*

1  **Listen and sing. Do karaoke.**

I have ✹ hair, and my ⊙ are red.
I have a blue 💧 and a ✹ head.

2 **Draw and color. Say, listen, and draw.**

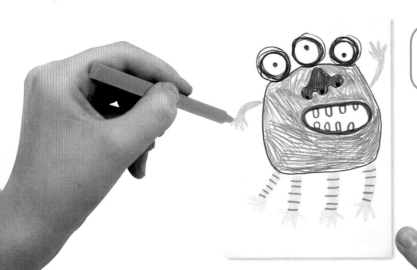

I'm a very ugly monster. I have three eyes.

1 🎧 73 ▶ **Watch and say.**

One tooth, two teeth, three teeth in Mrs. Monster's mouth.

2 **Say and guess.**

I have three small teeth.

Monster four!

1

2

3

4

Write it with me!

2 wo   **3** ree

1 🎧 74 ▶ **Watch the video.**

2 🎧 75 **Listen and say "yes" or "no."**

Marie's science

How do we use our senses?

1 ▶ **Watch and answer.**

2 🎧 76 **Listen and point.**

3 **Point and say.**

Eyes.   I see with my eyes.

We taste with our mouth. A butterfly tastes with its feet!

Fact

Project

Use your senses!

Trevor's values

Take care of pets

1 🎧 77 **Listen and say the number.**

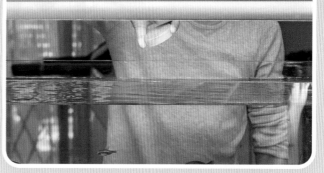

2 **Do the actions. Guess.**

You feed your fish.   Yes, that's right!

7 Wild animals

1 🎧 78–79 **Listen and point. Listen and repeat.**

bear

giraffe

elephant

snake

crocodile

monkey

hippo

tiger

2 **Play and say.**

It's big and gray.

It's an elephant!

Vocabulary presentation: animals

1  80 Listen and say the chant. Do the actions.

Tiger, elephant, hippo, snake,
Giraffe, bear, and crocodile.

2  81 Listen and point. Answer.

hand

leg

tail

arm

foot

feet

2 **Play and say.** They have big heads and small ears.

Hippos.

Language presentation and practice 1: *have* for possession *They have (short legs). They don't have (big heads).*

1  Listen and sing. Do karaoke.

Let's all do the 🦛 show. Let's all do the 🐘 dance.
Let's all do the 🐊 smile. Let's all do the 🦒 laugh!

2 Act it out and say.

What am I?   You're an elephant.

Language presentation and practice 2: *Let's do (the crocodile smile).*   51

Monty's sounds and spelling

1 🎧 86 ▶ **Watch and say.**

Six little pink hippos in the river.
He's the big hippo king.

2 **Ask and answer. Guess.**

It has a long tail.   A tiger.

Write it with me!

l_ttle
h_ppo

7

1  Watch the video.

 # 2 Act out the story.

8 My clothes

MASKMAN

1 🎧 88–89 **Listen and point. Listen and repeat.**

cap

skirt

T-shirt

jacket

socks   shoes

pants   shorts

2 **Play and say.**

Pants.

They're gray.

Vocabulary presentation: clothes

1 🎵🎧 90 Listen and say the chant.

I have blue pants
And a green T-shirt.
I have a brown jacket
And a purple skirt.

2 🎧 91 Listen and say the number.

Does Scott have my red pants?

2 **Say and guess.**

She has white shoes.
She doesn't have blue pants.

Joana!

Language presentation: *have* for possession *Do you/Does he/she have (my blue T-shirt)? He/She doesn't have (red shorts).*

 Listen and correct.

He has a 🌑 👕 in his hands, a 🌑 👕 in his hands.
She has a 🌑 ✏️ in her hands, a 🌑 ✏️ in her hands.

2 🎵🎧 95–96 ▶ Listen and sing. Do karaoke.

1 🎧 97 ▶ **Watch and say.**

Six snakes in T-shirts.

Seven sheep in socks and shoes.

2 **Say and guess.**

They have red T-shirts.

Monkeys!

Write it with me!

___ix ___oes

1 🎧 98 ▶ **Watch the video.**

8

1

2

3

4

5

2 🎧 99 **Listen and say the number.**

marie's geography

Where do animals live?

1 ▶ **Watch and answer.**

2 🎧 100 **Listen and match.**
Write the number.

1 lion
2 penguin
3 fox
4 polar bear
5 snail
6 bug
7 zebra

1

3 **Look, say, and guess.**

It lives in the garden.   A bug.

garden   polar region   savanna

The biggest land mammal is the elephant, and it lives in the savanna.

Fact

Project

Make a birdhouse.

Trevor's values

Love nature

1 🎧 101 **Listen and write the number.**

2 **Mime and guess.** Plant a tree. Yes!

1 102 **Listen and say the number.**

2 **Look, read, and match. Say.** It's a hippo.

polar bear   hippo   zebra   lion

3 **Play and say.**

They're eyes!

Finish

Start

9 Fun time!

play basketball

play the piano

play the guitar

swim

play tennis

play soccer

ride a bike

2 **Play the game.**

Simon says play the piano.

1 🎧 105 **Listen and answer.**

Ride a . Play , basketball.
Play, play, play!
Now let's ____. Play , the .
Play, play, play!

2 🎵🎧 106–107 ▶ **Listen and sing. Do karaoke.**

1 🎧 108–109 ▶ **Listen and point. Listen and repeat.**

I can't sing.

I can ride a bike.

She can ride a horse.

2 **Say and guess.**

She can't sing.

Sally.

Language presentation: *can* for ability *I/You can (swim). He/She can't (sing).*

1  **Listen and say the chant.**

I can play soccer, and I can drive my car.
I can't ride a bike, I can't swim.

2 **Ask and answer.**

Can you ride a bike?   Yes, I can.

Language practice: *can* for ability *Can you (play soccer)? Yes, I can. No, I can't.*   67

monty's sounds and spelling

1 🎧 111 ▶ **Watch and say.**

It's a gray day –
a snail can play with the train.

2 **Ask and answer.**

What can you do on a gray day?

I can play a game.

Write it with me!

gr_____ sn___l

1 112 ▶ Watch the video.

2 Act out the story.

10 At the amusement park

plane

truck

motorcycle

boat

helicopter

bus

2 **Ask and answer.**

Is the truck blue?

No, it's red.

Vocabulary presentation: transportation

 **Listen and say the chant. Do the actions.**

> Helicopter, ship. Long, blue train.
> Motorcycle, truck. Bus and plane.

 Listen and answer.

Is the red car in the shoe? Yes, it is.

117–118 ▶ **Listen and point. Listen and repeat.**

What are you doing, Maskman?

I'm flying my plane.

2 Play and say.

What am I doing?

Walking!

Language presentation: present progressive for ongoing actions *What are you doing? I'm (riding a bike).*

1  Listen and sing. Do karaoke.

I'm riding on my 🏍️.

I'm flying in my 🚁.

2 Do the actions. Ask and answer.

Are you driving a truck? No, I'm not.

Are you driving a car? Yes, I am!

Language practice: present progressive for ongoing actions *Are you (driving a car)? Yes, I am. / No, I'm not.* 73

Monty's sounds and spelling

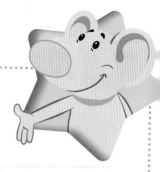

1 🎧 121 ▶ **Watch and say.**

Singing a song and swinging along.

Jumping and clapping all day long.

2 **Do the actions. Find and say.**

What am I doing?

You're singing a song.

Write it with me!

singi

1 🎧 122 ▶ **Watch the video.**

2 🎧 123 **Listen and say the number.**

Story: unit language in context   75

marie's geography

How do we travel?

 1 ▶ **Watch and answer.**

 2 🎧 124 **Listen and match.**

1 ship	4 scooter
2 monorail	5 van
3 hot-air balloon	

 3 **Look and complete.**

> helicopter   scooter   ship   van
> hot-air balloon   monorail

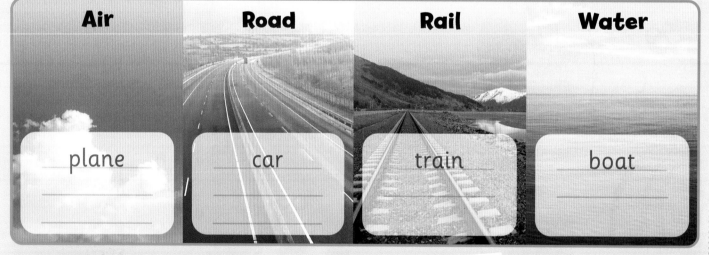

Air	Road	Rail	Water
plane	car	train	boat
___	___	___	___
___	___	___	___

Some cars can travel on the water.

Fact

Project

Design your own transportation.

Trevor's values

Work together

1 🎧 125 **Listen and say the number.**

2 🎧 126 **Listen and say. Act it out.**

11 Our house

bedroom

bathroom

living room

dining room

kitchen

hallway

2 **Ask and answer.**

Who's in the kitchen?

Sally.

Vocabulary presentation: the home

1  Listen and correct.

Monty's in the bathroom.

No, he isn't.
He's in the bedroom.

2  Listen and answer. Say the chant.

In the kitchen. In the dining room.
On the bathroom floor.
In the bedroom. In the living room.
Rolling down the hall.

Where's the video game?

It's in the living room.

1 🎧 132–133 ▶ **Listen and point. Listen and repeat.**

He's drawing a picture.

What's Scott doing?

2 **Play and say.**

Sally's riding a bike.

No. She's reading.

Language presentation: present progressive for ongoing actions *What's he/she doing? He's/She's (drawing a picture).*

1  Listen and sing. Do karaoke.

Where's 🧒? In her ___.

What's she doing? She's reading a ___.

2 Ask and answer.

What's Sally doing?

She's reading a book.

Where is she?

She's in the bedroom.

Language practice: present progressive for ongoing actions *What's he/she doing? He's/She's (playing the guitar).*   81

1 🎧 136 ▶ **Watch and say.**

**Monkey's riding a motorcycle in the bedroom.
Mouse is swimming in the bathroom.**

2 **Ask and answer.**

Where's Monkey?

He's in the bathroom.

What's he doing?

Write it with me!

bedroo

1 🎧 137 ▶ Watch the video.

2 🎧 138 Listen and say "yes" or "no."

Story: unit language in context

12 Party time!

happy birthday

fish

cake

ice cream

burger

apple

banana

chocolate

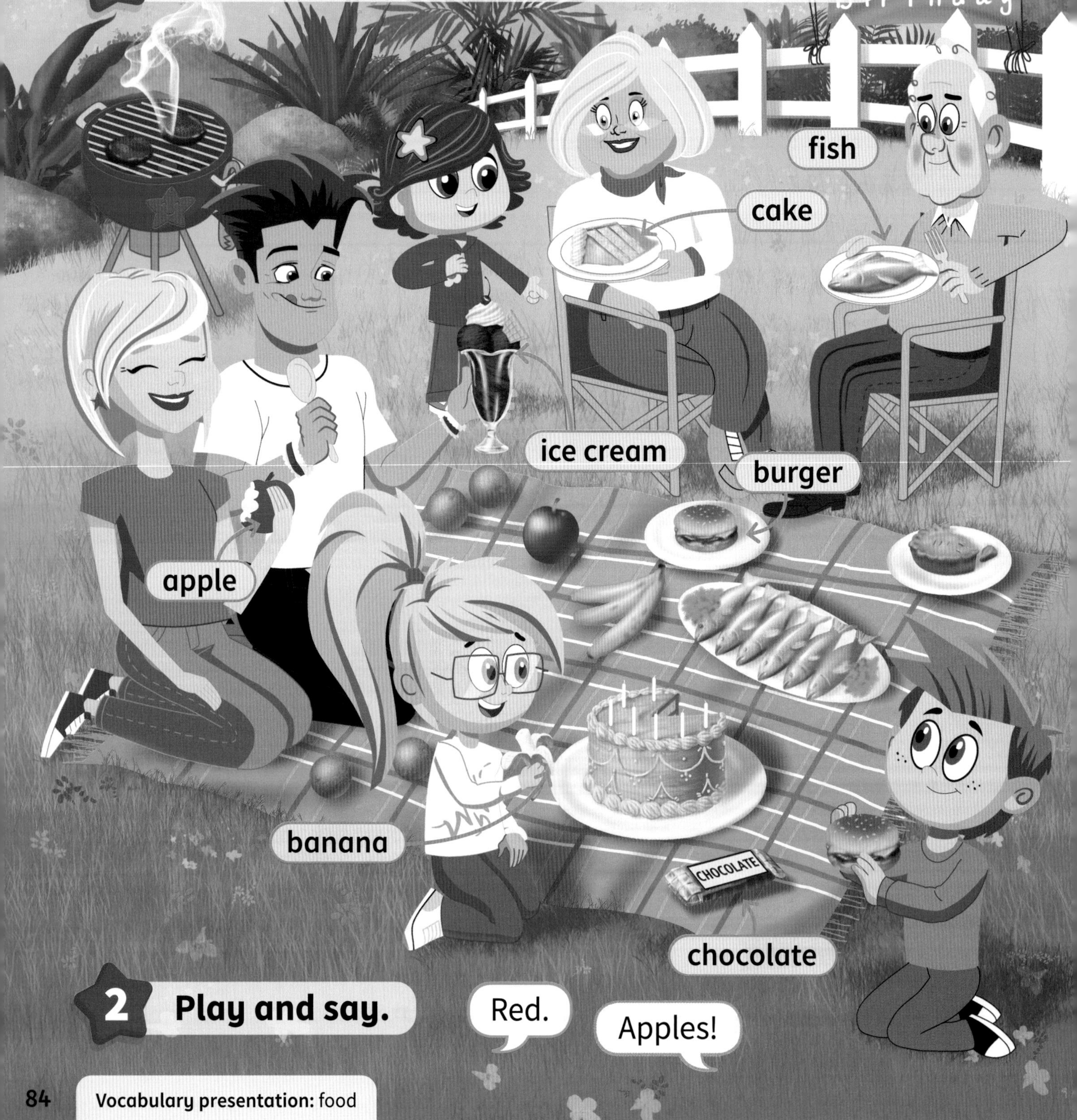

2 **Play and say.** Red. Apples!

1 ♪ 🎧 141 Say the chant.

Kiwi and cake.
Ice cream and chocolate.

2 🎧 142 Listen and say "yes" or "no."

1 🎧 143–144 ▶ **Listen and point. Listen and repeat.**

I like chocolate cake.

I don't like chocolate.

Do you like Maskman cake?

2 **Play and say.**

I like apples.

I like apples and bananas.

I like apples, bananas, and cake.

Language presentation: present simple *Do you like (fish)? I like (apples). I don't like (cake).*

1 🎵🎧 145-146 ▶ Sing the song. Do karaoke.

Do you like 🍌? Yes, yes, yes!
Do you like 🐟? Yes, yes, yes!
Do you like 🍔? Yes, yes, yes!

2 Ask and answer.

Do you like apples?　　Yes, I do.

Do you like ice cream?　　No, I don't.

Language practice: present simple *Do you like (ice cream)? Yes, I do. / No, I don't.*　87

Monty's sounds and spelling

1 🎧 147 ▶ **Watch and say.**

> *Three purple hippos swimming along.*
> *A red snake with big teeth in a hat.*
> *Doll, robot, and teddy bear singing a song.*
> *A boy playing with a mouse, a sheep, and a cat.*

2 **Play and say.**

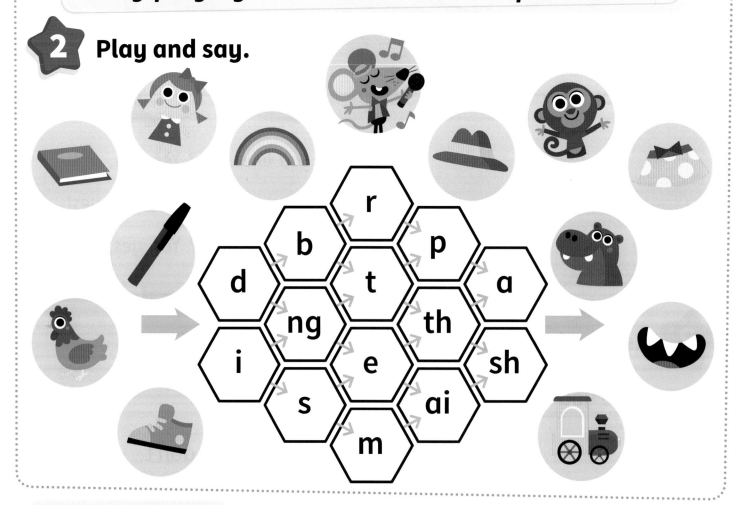

r

b   p

d   t   a

ng   th

i   e   sh

s   ai

m

88   Sounds and spelling: review

148 ▶ **Watch the video.**

 Act out the story.

Story: unit language in context   89

Marie's science

How do we grow fruit?

1 ▶ **Watch and answer.**

2 🎧 149 **Listen, point, and say.**

3 ▶ **Look, complete, and say.**

Apples grow on trees.

Apples grow in cold places.

Fruit	Tree	Ground	Hot place	Cold place
🍎	✓			✓
🥝				
🍉				
🍐				
🍓				
🍊				

This is called Ugli fruit because it's – ugly!

Fact

Project

Grow fruit.

Science: grow fruit | 🛡 learning to learn

Trevor's values

Keep clean

1 🎧 150 **Listen and point.**

2 🎵🎧 151 **Listen and say the chant. Do the actions.**

1 🎧 152 **Listen and answer.**

2 **Read.**

I'm Ben. I'm **7** . I like ⚽ and 🏐 ,
but I don't like 🎤 . I can 🏊 and ride a 🚲 ,
but I can't play the 🎸 . I like 🍰 and 🍔 ,
but I don't like 🍫 or 🍦 . I like 🍎
and 🍪 . I'm eating a 🍌 now.

3 Play and say.

They're playing basketball.

Grammar reference

| What's your name? | I'm Suzy. |
| How old are you? | I'm three. |

what's = what is   I'm = I am

Who's that?	That's Alex.
How old is he/she?	He's/She's seven.
How are you?	I'm fine, thank you.

who's = who is   that's = that is   he's = he is   she's = she is

| Where's your ball? | It's next to the chair. It isn't under the table. |
| Is your ball in your bag? | Yes, it is. No, it isn't. |

where's = where is   it's = it is   isn't = is not

| He's happy. | He isn't ugly. |

| They're long. | It's dirty. |

they're = they are

| I / You / We have a blue nose. | |
| Do you have a small mouth? | Yes, I do. No, I don't. |

don't = do not

7

They have big heads.	They don't have long legs.
Let's do the elephant dance.	

let's = let us

8

She has your red pants.	He doesn't have a blue T-shirt.
Does he have my red pants?	

doesn't = does not

9

I can ride a bike.	She can't sing.
Can you chant?	

can't = cannot

10

What are you doing?	I'm flying.
Are you riding a bike?	Yes, I am. No, I'm not.

11

What's he doing? What's she doing?	He's drawing a picture She's reading a book.

12

I like chocolate cake.	I don't like chocolate.
Do you like apples?	Yes, I do. No, I don't.

Animal House Museum

Starters Listening

1 🎧 153 **Listen. Who's at school today? Put a ✓ or an ✗ in the box.**

	📅		📅
Alex	✗	May	
Alice	✓	Nick	
Bill		Lucy	
Grace		Sam	
Kim		Tom	

2 🎧 154 🐵 **Listen and draw lines. There is one example.**

Alex   Sam   Alice   Matt

Kim   Lucy   Eva

Starters Listening

In picture 1, the guitar is next to the bed. In picture 2, the guitar is next to the door.

1 🎧 155 **Look at picture 1 and listen. Say "yes" or "no." Talk about the two pictures.**

2 🎧 156 🐵 **Listen and color. There is one example.**

Starters Reading and Writing

1 Read and look at your classroom. Say "yes" or "no."

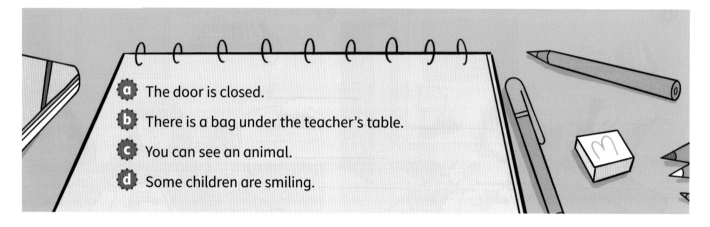

a The door is closed.

b There is a bag under the teacher's table.

c You can see an animal.

d Some children are smiling.

2 Look and read. Write "yes" or "no."

Examples

The bedroom door is open.	yes
The boy is smiling.	no

Questions

1 There is a green T-shirt on the chair.

2 The girl has a bag.

3 The boy is jumping on the bed.

4 The shoes and socks are under the chair.

5 The children are playing tennis.

Starters Reading and Writing

1 🕐 **Do the word puzzles. You have 3 minutes!**

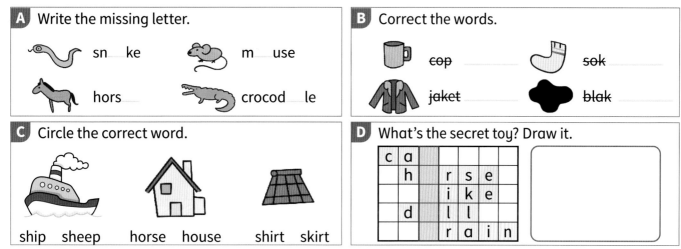

A Write the missing letter.

snke   muse

hors   crocodle

B Correct the words.

~~cop~~   ~~sok~~

~~jaket~~   ~~blak~~

C Circle the correct word.

ship   sheep   horse   house   shirt   skirt

D What's the secret toy? Draw it.

c	a				
	h		r	s	e
			i	k	e
	d		l	l	
			r	a	i	n

2 🐵 **Look at the pictures. Look at the letters. Write the words.**

Example

m o u s e

m
u   e
o   s

Questions

1 n
o   i   l

2 r   i
d
b

3 h   i
p   o
p

4 r   t
g
e   i

5 m   k   n
e   y   o

Starters Speaking

1 **Listen to your teacher. Play the game.**

2 🎧 157 **Listen and draw.**

① ② ③ ④

Pre A1 Starters Exam folder: Speaking Parts 1 and 2

1 🎧 158 Look and listen. Follow the instructions.

2 🎧 159 Listen. Put your cards on the picture.

3 🎧 160 Listen. Answer questions about the zoo.

Thanks and Acknowledgments

The authors and publishers acknowledge the following sources of copyright material and are grateful for the permissions granted. While every effort has been made, it has not always been possible to identify the sources of all the material used, or to trace all copyright holders. If any omissions are brought to our notice, we will be happy to include the appropriate acknowledgments on reprinting and in the next update to the digital edition, as applicable.

Key: U = Unit

General

Many thanks to everyone at Cambridge University Press & Assessment for their dedication and hard work, and in particular to:
Liane Grainger and Lynn Townsend for supervising the whole project and guiding us calmly through the storms;
Alison Bewsher for her keen editorial eye, enthusiasm, and great suggestions;
Zara Hutchinson-Goncalves for her energy, enthusiasm, and helpful suggestions.

We would also like to thank all our students and colleagues, past, present, and future, at Star English academy in Murcia, especially Jim Kelly for his friendship and support throughout the years.

This is for Lydia and Silvia, my own "stars," with all my love. – CN

For Paloma, for her love, encouragement, and unwavering support. Thanks. – MT

The authors and publishers acknowledge the following sources of copyright material and are grateful for the permissions granted. While every effort has been made, it has not always been possible to identify the sources of all the material used, or to trace all copyright holders. If any omissions are brought to our notice, we will be happy to include the appropriate acknowledgments on reprinting and in the next update to the digital edition, as applicable.

Photography

The following photos are sourced from Getty Images.

U1: Anna Erastova/iStock/Getty Images Plus; **U2:** Dimitri Otis/Stone; legalALIEN/DigitalVision Vectors; Eratel/DigitalVision Vectors; Thoth_Adan/DigitalVision Vectors; Bobby Coutu/E+; LightFieldStudios/iStock/Getty Images Plus; Ariel Skelley/DigitalVision; manonallard/E+; hadynyah/E+; Godruma/iStock/Getty Images Plus; EkaterinaKu/iStock/Getty Images Plus; aldarinho/iStock/Getty Images Plus; Anna Erastova/iStock/Getty Images Plus; **U3:** Anna Erastova/iStock/Getty Images Plus; **U4:** Mark Garlick/Science Photo Library; Samantha T. Photography/Moment; Carol Yepes/Moment; Andersen Ross Photography Inc/DigitalVision; Shingo Tosha/AFLO; Klaus Vedfelt/DigitalVision; picture/iStock/Getty Images Plus; Tim Robberts/DigitalVision; yozachika/iStock/Getty Images Plus; Pongnathee Kluaythong/EyeEm; Nednapa Chumjumpa/EyeEm; FreedomMaster/iStock/Getty Images Plus; broeb/iStock/Getty Images Plus; GlobalStock/E+; Jordan Siemens/Stone; Thomas Barwick/DigitalVision; Stockbyte; skynesher/iStock/Getty Images Plus; moch alfik indarto/iStock/Getty Images Plus; frimages/iStock/Getty Images Plus; Anna Erastova/iStock/Getty Images Plus; **U6:** Jose Luis Pelaez Inc/DigitalVision; Barbara Friedman/Moment; sharply done/E+; Geri Lavrov/Moment Open; J Shepherd/Photodisc; Lorianne Ende/EyeEm; Jim Cumming/Moment; Mint Images - Jamel Toppin/Mint Images RF; paul mansfield photography/Moment Open; Comstock/Stockbyte; vladans/iStock/Getty Images Plus; kobbydagan/iStock Editorial/Getty Images Plus; **U8:** Ingunn B. Haslekaas/Moment; Achim Mittler, Frankfurt am Main/Moment; Westend61; John Seaton Callahan/Moment; Paul Souders/Stone; Yuriy_Kulik/iStock/Getty Images Plus; Matteo Colombo/Moment; Rosemary Calvert/Stone; goinyk/iStock/Getty Images Plus; Ghislain & Marie David de Lossy/The Image Bank; 35007/E+; DmyTo/iStock/Getty Images Plus; RuslanDashinsky/E+; Jamie Grill/The Image Bank; Jose Luis Pelaez Inc/DigitalVision; Fat Camera/E+; snipes213/iStock/Getty Images Plus; kuritafsheen/RooM; Adam McGrath/500px Prime; David Talukdar/Moment; Leon Woods/EyeEm; Tobias Ackeborn/Moment; JGI; MariaTkach/iStock/Getty Images Plus; Kinwun/iStock/Getty Images Plus; Mike Schultz/EyeEm; RusN/iStock/Getty Images Plus; JackF/iStock/Getty Images Plus; Olga Gillmeister/iStock/Getty Images Plus; DeluXe-PiX/iStock/Getty Images Plus; Aukid Phumsirichat/EyeEm; gofotograf/iStock/Getty Images Plus; Somsak Bumroongwong/EyeEm; Jurmin Tang/EyeEm; ivanastar/E+; Ryan McVay/DigitalVision; GlobalP/iStock/Getty Images Plus; Indeed; heinteh/iStock/Getty Images Plus; amriphoto/E+; Dmytro_Skorobogatov/iStock/Getty Images Plus; hayatikayhan/iStock/Getty Images Plus; Poh Kim Yeoh/EyeEm; Roberto Peradotto/Moment; Morsa Images/DigitalVision; imagenavi; Emely/Cultura; **U10:** Henglein And Steets/Photolibrary; Carl & Ann Purcell/The Image Bank Unreleased; Vacclav/iStock/Getty Images Plus; avid_creative/E+; MichaelSvoboda/iStock/Getty Images Plus; Xuanyu Han/Moment; mikroman6/Moment; prospective56/iStock/Getty Images Plus; Jaris Ho/Moment; AlasdairJames/iStock Unreleased; NathanMarx monkeybusinessimages/iStock/Getty Images Plus; BJI/Blue Jean Images; Norbert Schaefer/Corbis; SDI Productions/iStock/Getty Images Plus; **U12:** Image Source; Adina Tovy/Lonely Planet Images; Patrick Johns/Corbis/VCG/Corbis Documentary; EdwardSamuelCornwall/iStock/Getty Images Plus; Mr. Patipat Rintharasri/EyeEm; Tom Eversley/EyeEm; Akepong Srichaichana/EyeEm; Creativ Studio Heinemann; Richard Clark/The Image Bank; Anastassios Mentis/Photolibrary; BJI/Blue Jean Images; Dorling Kindersley: Will Heap; vasilis ververidis/500px; Randy Mayor/Photographer's Choice RF; WP Simon/Photodisc; Bignai/iStock/Getty Images Plus; Westend61; zentilia/iStock/Getty Images Plus; rubberball; Jade Albert Studio, Inc./Stone; izusek/E+; ziggy_mars/iStock/Getty Images Plus; Saturated/iStock/Getty Images Plus; Indeed; Image Source/Photodisc; OJO Images/Justin Pumfrey/Photolibrary; NickBiemans/iStock/Getty Images Plus; Meggj/iStock/Getty Images Plus; Torsten Blackwood/AFP; SW Productions/Stockbyte; Tosaphon C/500px Prime; Weedezign/iStock/Getty Images Plus; Delta Images/Image Source.

The following photos are sourced from other libraries.

U2: Gino Santa Maria/Shutterstock; **U12:** Wavebreak Media ltd/Alamy Stock Photo.

Commissioned photography by Trevor Clifford Photography.

Illustrations

Beth Hughes (The Bright Agency); Chants; Clara Soriano (The Bright Agency); Dan Crisp (The Bright Agency); Gaby Zermeno (Direct artist); Jake McDonald (The Bright Agency); Matthew Scott (The Bright Agency); Marek Jagucki; Pronk Media Inc.

Video

Video acknowledgements are in the Teacher Resources on Cambridge One.

Audio

Audio managed by Hyphen Publishing, produced by New York Audio Productions and John Marshall Media.

Songs composed by Robert Lee.

Design and typeset

Blooberry Design

Additional authors

Katy Kelly: Monty's Sounds and Spelling
Rebecca Legros: Marie's art, geography and science
Montse Watkin: Exam folders